Dented Breeze

Mark Cunningham

Dented Breeze
© 2023 by Mark Cunningham
All rights reserved.
Published by Mark Cunningham
ISBN 979-8-9882957-3-0

Thanks to Linda Kobert, Christopher Simmons, harry k stammer, Amy Stephenson, and Mark Young.

Cover photograph by Tim Mossholder on Unsplash.

TABLE OF CONTENTS

Ode to the Poetical Character
by William Collins   3

from *The Deserted Village, A Poem*
by Oliver Goldsmith   6

The Book of Thel
by William Blake   13

II

The Eolian Harp
by Samuel Taylor Coleridge   23

"England! the time is come when thou shouldst wean"
by William Wordsworth   26

"There is a bondage worse, far worse, to bear"
by William Wordsworth   27

"The world is too much with us; late and soon"
by William Wordsworth   28

London, 1802
by William Wordsworth   29

Composed Upon Westminster Bridge, September 3, 1802
by William Wordsworth   30

from Frost at Midnight
by Samuel Taylor Coleridge   31

III

Ode: Intimations of Immortality from
       Recollections of Early Childhood
by William Wordsworth   35

On First Looking into Chapman's Homer
by John Keats   43

from Childe Harold's Pilgrimage, Canto III
by George Gordon, Lord Byron   44

from Childe Harold's Pilgrimage, Canto III
by George Gordon, Lord Byron   45

Ode to the West Wind
by Percy Bysshe Shelley   47

"And did those feet in ancient times"
by William Blake   51

from Preface to Lyrical Ballads, with
       Pastoral and Other Poems
by William Wordsworth   52

from Biographia Literaria, chapter XIII
by Samuel Taylor Coleridge   53

from Letter to George and Tom Keats,
December 21-27, 1817
by John Keats   55

from Letter to George and Georgiana
        Keats, February 14-May 3, 1819
by John Keats   56

IV

from *Milton*
by William Blake   61

from The Rime of the Ancient Mariner
by Samuel Taylor Coleridge   65

Prometheus
by George Gordon, Lord Byron   67

from *Frankenstein; or, the Modern
        Prometheus*
by Mary Shelley   69

Nutting
by William Wordsworth   71

Ode to a Nightingale
by John Keats   73

from Preface to Kubla Khan, or, A Vision
        in a Dream: A Fragment
by Samuel Taylor Coleridge   77

from *Alastor; or, the Spirit of Solitude*
by Percy Bysshe Shelley   79

V

from *Don Juan*, Canto IX
by George Gordon, Lord Byron   89

Dented Breeze

I

Ode to the Poetical Character
by William Collins

I

The German word *Herz* means heart,
       cour
Age, mind, spirit, feeling, core. The heart
In a fetus develops
18 to 22 days after the
Egg is fertilized. The human
Fetus develops out of the
Embryo, which shares character
Istics with embryos of oth

Er species: for instance, the first flesh
Y fold at the base of a human and
A shark embryo's head both develop
Into jaw bones. The earliest known
      sharks
Date from over 420 mil
Lion years ago. The Silurian
Period covers the years from 443.7
Million to 416 million years
Ago, and also saw the stabili
Zation of the earth's climate and the ap
Pearance of Cooksonia, the first vas
Cular plant, on land. Sir Roder
Ick Impen Murichison, who was born
At Tarradale House, Muir of Ord, Ross-
      Shire, Scot

II

Land, named the Silurian Pe

Riod after the Silures tribe
Of Wales. The Ross-shire area
Is renowned for its spectacu
Lar mountain scenery. The world's
Largest mountain ranges—the Alps
And the Himalaya, for in
Stance—consist of fold mountains, form
Ed when two tectonic plates col
Lide head-on and the crumbled ed
Ges of the plates buckle. Mt. Ev
Erest, a mountain in the Him
Alayan range, is the world's tall
Est mountain, reaching 20,029
Feet above sea level. On May
16, 1975
Junko Tabei became the first
Woman to reach the sum
Mit of Mt. Everest. In 1975
The Lever Brothers introduced
Aim toothpaste, a fluoridated gel,
To supplement their Pepsodent and
Close-Up brands. The free element
Fluorine is not found naturally
On earth, but only in plan
Etary nebulae, stars, and
The interstellar medium (the matter
Between star systems in a gal
Axy). An expanding shell of
Ionized gas, a planetar
Y nebula returns car
Bon, nitrogen, calcium, and

III

Other elements to space. Much
Of the nitrogen in our at

Mosphere came from gas escaping
From the molten Earth, and some still
Enters that way today during
Volcanic eruptions. Five vol
Canoes—Kohala Huala
Lai, Mauna Kea, Mauna Lo
A—form the island of Hawaii.
Though many people associate
Hawaii with pineapples, the leading
    countries
For canned pineapple production are
    Puer
To Rico, Mexico, Guinea, Ivory
Coast, and Martinique. Taiwan, the
Philippines, and South Africa are
Among the leading producers of canned
    and
Fresh pineapple. Pineapple is a tast
Y and popular ingredi
Ent in ice cream and tropical
Fruit salads. Chocolate ice cream,
The most popular flavor other than van
Illa, according to the International

from *The Deserted Village, A Poem*
by Oliver Goldsmith

ll. 35-74

Ice Cream Association, was first pro
Duced in France in 1533 when
A chef added flavors such as choco
Late to ice milk—though the recipe is
Thought to have come originally from
Italy. In 1533, Cath
Erine de Medici married the fu
Ture Henry II of France. Cath
Erine's great-grandfather Lorenzo de
Medici, surrounded himself with art
Ists and philosophers such as Leo
Da Vinci, Sandro Botticelli, Domen
Ico Ghirlandaio, Michelangelo,
Marsilio Ficino, and Gio
Vanni Pico della Mirandola.
In his notes, Leonardo states that wat

Ter "readily raises itself by heat in
Thin vapor through the air. Cold causes it
To freeze. Stagnation makes it foul." *The
Birth of Venus* by Botticelli
Shows the goddess standing in a shell
      blown
Toward the shore. The atmosphere of

The planet Venus was first detected
In 1761 by the as
Tronomer and poet Mikhail Lomon
Sov. Lomonsov's *Ode on the Taking of
Khotin from the Turks* was highly regard

Ed when it appeared in 1739.

According to the ode, "Even the slight
Est trembling leaf / Strikes fear into their
    [the
Tartars'] hearts now / Like screaming
    cannon
Balls." Wind that would cause the
    slightest trem
Bling of a leaf would probably rank ei
Ther a 1 (1-3 m.p h.)
Or a 2 (2-4 m.p h.)
On the Beaufort scale. Originally,
The Beaufort scale measured not wind
    speed di
Rectly, but its effects on the sea sur
Face or the sails of a man-of-war, which
Was then the main ship of the British Roy

ll. 113-136

Al Navy. The highest officer rank
In the Royal Navy is Admiral
Of the Fleet, though the rank was
    abolished
In the 1990s, and only those
Who had already attained the rank were
Allowed to continue to hold it. Be
Tween 1718 and 1739,
The most senior Admiral held this ti
Tle even if there was no fleet in ex
Istence for him to command. In 17
39, the War of Jenkin's Ear
Breaks out between England and Spain
    af
Ter English mariner Robert Jenkins

Starts a barroom brawl with a Spanish
               Customs
Guard in Havana and receives a cut
To the ear that leads to the ear's am
Putation; Jenkins keeps the ear, and a
Member of Parliament waves it in the
House of Commons while demanding
               revenge
For the mistreatment of British smugglers
And pirates. 16,000 to 20,
000 inner hair cells in the ear are
The link between the organ of Cor
Ti and the central nervous system which
               trans

ll. 265-286

Mits signals to the brain, where they are
               inter
Preted as sounds. Human hearing can
Hear sounds ranging from 15-20
To 16,000-20,000 hertz.
The hertz number equals the number of
Cycles per second, and hertz can be
               used
To measure sight as well as sound. Dogs,
               who
Have a temporal resolution of
60-70 hertz have trouble
Watching television, since modern
               screens
Run at 50-60 hertz. The tel
Evision show *Lassie* premiered on
CBS on September 12, 1954 and ran
For 588 episodes
Until March 24, 1973.

The CBS eye logo first appear
Ed on air on Saturday, October
20, 1951. William Gold
En, the eye's designer, said he was in
Spired in part by symbols resembling
The human eye that were drawn on the
    sides
Of Shaker barns to ward off evil spir

II. 309-362

Its. Anne Lee, one of the founders of
The Shakers, had four children die in in
Fancy and claimed several reve
Lations relating the fall of Adam
And Eve to sexual intercourse; the
Group's rejection of sexual inti
Macy lead to a steady decline in
Membership, and as of December, 2
009, only three members remain
Ed. In Christian numerological
Symbolism, three is the number of
Divine Perfection, since the Trinity
Consists in the Father, the Son, and the
    Ho
Ly Ghost, and the universe is made of
Space, time, and matter. Though he
    claimed
To form no hypothesis, Isaac New
Ton believed that the cause of gravity—
    which
Is non-material, since it would be
Impossible for one corpuscular
Particle of matter to affect an
Other particle directly and phys
Ically with void space between them—is

The action of the spirit of God. The
Wall note for Alexander Ross's paint
Ing *Untitled* in the Nelson-Atkins
Museum of Art in Kansas City,
Missouri, claims the canvas depicts "an or
Ganic, corpuscular form hovering

Before a blue sky," though what exactly
This entity is "remains elusive"—
Though it looks to be a cluster of frozen
Peas. Peas were included in Swanson's
      first

Frozen dinner, along with turkey, dress
Ing, and sweet potatoes, as well as its
Third (mixed vegetables, with fried
Chicken and mashed potatoes). 1960:
apple cobbler. But Swanson's frozen Sau
Erbraten, Bavarian red cabbage,
And spaetzle frozen dinner was intro
Duced in the late 1950s, but failed,
Supposedly over lingering re
Sentment of Germany over World War
II. While the origin of the Final
Solution—the mass killing of Jewish
People by Nazis or their allies at
Specifically designed extermina
Tion camps—is often given as the
Wannsee Conference held in Januar
Y 1942, some histori
Ans argue for moving the date to
Late 1941, with the killing
Of Jewish men, women, and children
By Ukrainian civilians and mili
Tia units at the Janovska camp

ll. 395-430

At Lvov, or the activity of
Nazi mobile killing units in Kau
Nas, Lithuania on June 2
5, 1941. The narrator
Of Alain Renais's 1955 film *Night
And Fog*, which combines black and
    white doc
Umentary footage of the concen
Tration camps with color images of
The camps in decay a decade af
Ter the war's end, says, "We pretend it all
    hap
Pened only once, at a given time and
Place. We turn a blind eye to what
    surrounds
Us." The assistant director of *Night and
    Fog*,
Chris Marker, was born Christian
    Francois
Bouche-Velleneuve and took the name
Marker from the Magic Marker felt tip
Pen. In New Zealand, the generic term
For felt-tip markers is "felts." For over
Thirty years, I thought the country direct
Ly above Australia on the maps was
New Zealand rather than New Guinea.
    Rug
By League is considered the national
Sport of New Guinea. One of the main dif
Ferences between rugby league and rug
By union rules is that the rugby league
Matches are played under the 6-tac
Kle rule, meaning that the ball-holding
    team

11

May be tackled only six times before hav
ing to hand over possession of the
Ball, while in rugby union a team may
Retain possession of the ball for as
Long as it is able. According to
Legend, the game of rugby was invent
Ed in 1823 at Rugby
School, when a student named William
           Webb
Ellis broke the rules of football by pick

The Book of Thel
by William Blake

PLATE i

THEL'S Motto,

Ing up the ball and running with it.
The headmaster at rugby
At the time was John Wool; he was suc
Ceeded by Thomas Arnold father of

PLATE 1

THEL

I

English writer Mathew Arnold. In 1832,
The elder Arnold bought Fox How, a
 small estate near Am
Bleside in the Lake District.
 Bassenthwaite Lake is the
Only body of water in the Lake District offi
Cially named a "lake"; the other bodies of
 water are

"Waters," "tarns," or "meres." In
 November 2009, heavy
Rains added 22,100,000,000 lit
Res of water to Windermere in 36 hours.
 From
1901 to 1964, a litre was de
Fined as the volume of one kilogram of
 pure water at

4 degrees Celsius and 760 milli
Meters of mercury pressure, though it is
    now defined
As a cubic decimeter. When mercury is
    depos
Ited in water, the actions of micro-
    organisms can change into meth

Ylmercury; a toxic form can build up in
    fish and shell
Fish, leading to mercury poisoning of
    those who eat them.
Symptoms of mercury poisoning include
    tremors, ex
Cessive shyness, and insomnia. One
    suggestion for cur
Ing insomnia in children is to remove the
    clocks from
Their bedrooms or to turn the clocks'
    faces so that the child can't
See them. According to Phillipe Aries,
    before the 17th
Century, children were represented in
    media such
As painting and school records as
    miniature adults.
The average height for an adult human
    male in the Pa
Leolithic period was 171.

PLATE 2

1 cm (5 ft. 10 inches). A statue of

Edward II of England dating from 132

4 gives the legal definition of an inch as "three grains
Of barley, dry and round, placed end to end, lengthwise." Derived from
The annual grass Hordeum vulgare, barley is a cere
Al with a rich nutlike flavor and a pasta-like con
sistency. In American slang, a "nut" is a per
Son suspected of having a mental illness. In the
Mid-twentieth century, a widely-used treatment for
Mental illness was electro-shock therapy, which Dr.
Lee Colman says produces physiological chang
Es in the human brain "completely consistent with an

Y acute brain injury such as a blow to the head from
A hammer." A hammer equipped with a titanium
Head has only about 3% recoil, compared to
One with a steel head, which has about 27%

Recoil, so a titanium-headed hammer can re
Sult in greater efficiency in converting mechanic

PLATE 3

II

AI work into kinetic energy. Titanium
Oxide bands are prominent in the spectra
    of M-type
Stars, which are the coolest stars, with
    surface temperatures
Less than 3,200 degrees Celsius. The

Celsius scale is named after the Swedish
    astrono
Mer Anders Celsius. The latitude and
    longitude of Stock

Holm, Sweden, is 59 degrees 20' 0"
N / 18 degrees 3' 0" E. At the 18
84 International Meridian Confer
Ence, the Dominican Republic was the
    only one
Of the twenty-five countries attending that
    voted against
The adoption of Greenwich, England, as
    the zero-longi
Tude line, from which all other longitudes
    would be calcu
Lated. In the Dominican Republic, August
    1
6 is Restoration Day, a non-working holi
Day commemorating the August 16, 186

3 raid on Santo Domingo by armed
    revolution
Aries that resulted in the raising of the
    Domini

Can flag on the capitol hill and the
   beginning of
The civil war that restored Dominican
   sovereign
Ty after its having been ceded back to
   Spain. The rub
Y is generally considered the birthstone
   of those
Born under the zodiac sign of Leo
   (roughly Ju

Ly 23-August 22); it is believed

To strengthen the physical and emotional
   heart,
To bring love, confidence, loyalty, and
   courage, and to
Instill stamina, vitality, and strength.
   Citrine crys
Tals have been claimed to open the third
   eye. H. P. Blavat
Sky claimed that the pineal gland is
   actually the third

Eye. Recent research has shown that the
   pineal gland is
The area of most intense concentration of
   fluor

PLATE 4

III

Ide in the body, which can result in the
   depression of

Melatonin synthesis and an earlier onset
Puberty in the female gerbil. *Meriones
Unguiculatus*, a gentle and hardy Mongo
Lian species, also known as the Clawed
Jird,
Was brought in the 19th century from
China to France,

Where it became a popular household
pet, and then to A
Merica in 1954 for research pur
Poses by Dr. Victor Schwentker. With
much of its

Area covered by steppes, mountains, and
the Gobi des
Ert, Mongolia is the most sparsely
populated
Independent country in the world. A
scientif

PLATE 5

Ic measurement-based definition of a
desert must
Consider not only rainfall amounts but
evap
Otranspiration rates (the combined loss
due to at
Mospheric evaporation and plant use) as
well as
The surface storage of water. Since it can
be solid,
(Ice), liquid, and gas, Thales of Miletus
thought water

Was the basis of all things. Jan Baptista
      van Helmont, a sev
Enteenth century Flemish chemist,
      introduced the word
"Gas," an alteration of the Greek "khaos"
      or empty
Space, into the scientific vocabulary.
      From
1826 to 1892, the Tu
Dor Ice Company of Boston shipped ice
      harvested in
New England to the Caribbean, Europe,
      and Indi

A. Boston's professional baseball team,
      the Red Sox, re
Ceived its spelling when it turned out
      "Stockings Win!" set in
Large type would not fit on the local
      newspaper's page as a
Headline. While Rome had daily
      handwritten news sheets posted

PLATE 6

IV

In the Forum from 59 B.C.E. to at
Least 222 C.E., among the
First printed forerunners of newspapers in
      Europe are
German broadsides and news pamphlets
      that appeared in the late
1400s and featured, among other
      sensation

Al items, reports of atrocities committed
by
Vlad Tespes Drakul against Germans in
Transylvania.
Bela Lugosi, who played Dracula in the
193
1 Hollywood film, used opiates, particular
Ly morphine, to offset the pain of chronic
sciat

Ica. Discovered in 1804 by Friedrich
Serturner, first sold commercially by
Merck in
1827, and more widely used
After the successful development of
The hypodermic needle in 1844,
morphine is named after
Morpheus, the Greek god of dreams. A
person who
Dreams that she is being chased by
Godzilla in K
Mart, and the Blue Light Special Light
comes on whenever she tries
To hide can be diagnosed as trying to run
from
Her problems, and the blue light may
represent her feelings of hope

Lessness. Godzilla's creation as a result
Of radiation from nuclear explosions
draws not on

II

The Eolian Harp
by Samuel Taylor Coleridge

Ly on Japanese memories of Hiro
Shima and Nagasaki, but also
New fears concerning the hydrogen
    bomb,
Since the fallout from the Castle Bravo
    test on
The Bikini Atoll on March 1, 19
54 fell on several tuna fish
Ing boats that were outside what was
    then
Considered the danger zone. Though orig
Inally named Eschscholtz Atoll in hon
Or of Johann Friedrich von Eschscholtz,
The first naturalist to describe the a
Corn worm, the native

Marshall Islanders
Called the atoll "Bikini," from the Mar
Shallese "pik," meaning "surface," and
    "ni,"
Meaning "coconut." Fresh coconut toddy
Is high in Vitamin C (one and a
Half cups provides 263
% of the daily Vitamin C
Requirement for an adult wo
Man), while green coconut water, the
Germinating coconut, and the heart
Of the coconut palm also have use
Ful amounts of Vitamin C. Linus Paul
Ing, who advocated Vitamin C
As a way to control the common cold
Is the only person to win two un
Divided Nobel Prizes, and, with Mar

le Curie, he is one of only two peo
Ple to win Prizes in separate fields, have
Ing been awarded the Nobel Prize in
Chemistry in 1954 and
The Nobel Peace Prize in 196
2. Marie Curie discovered two el

Ements, polonium and radium.
Though highly toxic, polonium was
Once used by makers of photographic
Plates, because the ionizing radi
Ation it emits allows static e
Lectricity to dissipate, reducing
The amount of dust attracted to the
Plates. One of Man Ray's most famous
      photo
Graphs, *Dust Breeding*, taken in January,
1920, shows thick dust that had gath

Ered on Marcel Duchamps's *Bride
      Stripped Bare by
Her Bachelors, Even* while it was stored
In Duchamp's studio, before the glass
Was cracked while in transit in 1927
After being exhibited at the

Brooklyn Museum. In Alexander Pope's
Rape of the Lock, allusions to cracked
Or broken china are often taken to
Indicate that the loss of the lock of
Hair involves not only the outraging
Of Belinda's narcissism, but al
So the loss of her virginity. In Pope's
Time, the main porcelain factory in
China was the imperial plant at
Jingdezhen, which employed some 3,000

Kilns for ceramics. The Qin dynasty ruled China between 1644 and 1912. The ABC tele
Vision show *Dynasty* won the Golden Globe Award for Best Television Dra
Ma in 1984, and it be

"England! the time is come when thou
         shouldst wean"
by William Wordsworth

Came the top-ranked show in 198
5. Esther Shapiro, co-creator
Of *Dynasty*, said the inspiration
For the program came from Robert
         Graves'
1934 novel *I, Claudi
Us*, which along with its sequel *Clau
Dius the God*, had itself been turned into
A popular television mini-
Series by the BBC in 19
76. Claudius, the first Ro
Man emperor born outside Ital
Y, ruled from 41 to 54
CE, and was notorious for speak
Ing with a stammer, though some have
         thought

"There is a bondage worse, far worse, to
    bear"
by William Wordsworth

He had Tourette's syndrome. Though
    George Albert
Edouard Brutus Gilles de la Tourette's 18
85 paper described nine patients
Who suffered from the syndrome that
    would be named af
Ter him, the name itself was given by
Jean-Martin Charcot, who included Sig
Mund Freud among his students.
    Charcot's name is
Associated with many diseases, in
Cluding Charcot's Disease, or amytro
Phic sclerosis, also known as Lou Geh
Rig's disease. Known as the Iron Horse
    or Bis
Cuit Pants, Lou Gehrig drove in 18
4 runs in 1931. In the U
Nited States, a "biscuit" refers to a

"The world is too much with us; late and
       soon"
by William Wordsworth

Small, soft leavened bread, while in
       England it
Refers to a small, hard flour-based
       product,
Similar to what would in the Uni
Ted States be termed a "cookie" or a
       "cracker." Though
No one is sure when or how the first leav
Ening of bread occurred, the earliest
Record of leavened bread is in Egyptian
Hieroglyphs over five thousand years old
       that
Depict bread rising next to ovens. The
Nature of Egyptian hieroglyphs re
Mained misunderstood until the discov
Ery of the Rosetta Stone by Napo
Leon's troops in 1799: the
Stone presents a text in hieroglyphic

London, 1802
by William Wordsworth

Demotic (a simplified popular
Glyph form), and Greek writing, which al
Lowed Jean-Francois Champollion to de
Cipher the text and to state that
        hieroglyphs
Are "figurative, symbolic, and phonet
Ic all at once." Worried by Napoleon's
Defeat of the Mameluke army in the
Battle of the Pyramids and the conse
Quent threat to British navel superi
Ority in the Mediterrane
An, Horatio Nelson met and defeated
The French fleet in the Battle of the Nile,
Fought from August 1-3, 17
98. Image 35a7

Composed Upon Westminster Bridge,
September 3, 1802
by William Wordsworth

2, taken by Viking I on July
25, 1976 as it
Orbited the planet Mars, shows a hill
That bears an uncanny resemblance
To a human face: this, as well as
Other formations that resemble pyr
Amids, have led some to theorize a
New of lost civilizations that once
Inhabited the planet; however, these
Structures disappeared over time, or in
More high-resolution photographs, turned
Out to be examples of parei
Dolia, a psychological phenom
Enon in which vague or random stim

from Frost at Midnight
by Samuel Taylor Coleridge

ll. 43-74

Uli are believed to be signifi
Cant. The Rorschach test, a series of ten
Cards marked with inkblots (five black,
    two black and
White, and three multicolored), depends
    on
Pareidolia to lure responses
That will reveal important psycholog
Ical patterns in the subjects. Card V
In the Rorschach series is most fre
Quently interpreted as a bat or
A moth, though really it is a small per
Son, maybe a child, wearing a bug suit
With over-long puffy sleeves that cannot
Hide the murderous pincher claws the fig
Ure has instead of normal human hands.
Allowing for a few exceptions, two
Of the main distinguishing differences
Between moths and butterflies are 1) that
While most butterflies have thin slender fil
Amentous antennae that are club-shaped
At the end, moths tend to have comb-like
    or
Feathery anennae, or filamen

Tous and unclubbed antennae, and 2) but
Terflies fly during the day and moths fly
    dur
Ing the night. Though the first successful
    light

Bulb filaments were made of carbonized
Paper or bamboo, most filaments are
Now made of tungsten. Very pure
    tungsten can
Be cut with a hacksaw. Most hand-held
    hack
Saws have a pistol grip. The Hussite
    Wars
(1419-1434)
Are often considered the first wars in

III

Ode: Intimations of Immortality from
      Recollections of Early Childhood
by William Wordsworth

Europe in which hand-held gun
Powder weapons, including the
Píšťala, a weapon from which the gen

I

Eral term "pistol" partly derives. Gun
Powder was known as early as
The 9th century
In China, and apparently
Was an offshoot of alchemical ex
Periments aimed at finding an elix
Ir for immortalit
Y. According to
Carl Jung, the alchemical virgin Mercuri

II

Us, though an analog
To the Virgin Mary
And the gnostic virgin
Of light, is hermaphroditic ow
Ing to the presence in its
Body of sulphur, the
Active male principle. NASA's Pro
Ject Mercury succeeded in
Making John Glenn the fifth person to fly
      in space

III

And the first American to orbit
The Earth. To commemor
Ate the Mercury Pro
Ject, the United States Post Office in
1962 issued a four-cent stamp.
The single known copy
Of the Swedish Three Skilling Banco,
      printed
By error in yellow rather than the
Normal green, sold at auction in 19
96 for $2.27
Million. The piece
Of gold that
Set off the gold rush is small and
Beaten into a square
About the thickness of the foil
Wrapper of a
Stick of chewing gum. John Curtis
      introduced the first com

IV

Mercial chewing gum, Maine Pure Spruce
      Gum, in
1848. The im
Mature cones of the Black Spruce are
      purple. Rho
Dopsin, also known as visu
Al purple, consists of a
A protein moiety called scotopsin, an op
Sin; opsins are G protein re
Ceptors with seven transmembrane
Domains that form a pock
et where the retinal (as

Photoreac
Tive chromophore) (absorbs color) binds
To lysine residue in the
Seventh transmembrane domain. If
    exposed
To light, the pigment photobleach
Es, resulting in a lowered
Ability to see in the dark. A
Mong marmosets, tamarins, and squirrel
And spider monkeys, the
Females can distinguish
Reds but the males can't. Tamarins
    normal
Ly give birth to twins. While Castor, the
    sec

V

Ond brightest "star" in the constellation
    Gem
Ini, looks to the unaided eye to
Be a single star, it is
Actually made up of
Three double stars. One of the first
Europeans to observe that
Mizar, the second star from the end of
The Big Dipper's han
Dle, is a double star, Giovanni
Battista Riccioli, was a Cath
Olic priest. The priesthood
Of the Catholic Church includes those of
    both
The Latin and the East
Ern Rite Churches. In the Eastern Rite
    Church, Lent
Begins on the Monday of the

Week of Ash Wednesday, rather
Than on Ash Wednesday itself.
While both the Roman and the British
Empires used a seven-day week, the
      French

VI

Calendar after the 178
9 revolution divided the month
Into three sets of ten days, while after the
1917 Rus
Sian revolution, Russia
Adopted the Gregorian cal
Endar, which divided the year
Into 72 five-day weeks, three of

VII

Which were split into two partial weeks by
Five national holidays, with the two
Split weeks still totaling five days each.
Film director Dziga Vertov was not
      pleased
When Lenin began to allow foreign
Films into the Soviet Union: Ver
Tov noted that these films were nearly
Always fictional dramas represent
Ing a bourgeois individu
Alistic world view, as oppose
Ed to communistic
Documentaries, such as his
Own *Man with a Movie
Camera* and *Three Songs About Lenin*,
Which Vertov believed pre
Sented a more accu

Rate view of the world. Most
People are affected by change
    blindness—
They do not recognize abrupt changes
Made during the 30 milliseconds
Or so of a saccadic eye movement—
To the extent that John Grimes
Has shown that many viewers

VIII

Do not notice that characters have
    changed
Heads. The smallest measure
Of time possible according to
Current theories is one Planck time,
Which is the time it would take a photon
Traveling at the speed of light to cross
    one
Planck length (about 10^{-20}
The size of a proton):
This would take 10^{-43}
Seconds. One of 80 institutes in
The Max Planck Society, the Max Planck
Institute for Biological Cy
Bernetics is located in Tübin
Gen. If a word has two vowels, one spo
Ken with the tongue far back in the mouth
And the other with the tongue far forward,
Pronunciation can be difficult, so
Starting c. 450-500
C. E., various German languag
Es began the process of umlauting,
Or, with few exceptions, changing the pro

IX

Nunciation of the back
Vowel to make it clos
Er to that of the front vow
El. Rimbaud's sonnet "Voy
Elles" which includes the line "U, waves,
    divine
Shudderings of veridian seas," is of
Ten given as a prime example of
Synesthesia, the overflow of the
Perception of one sense into that
Of another. A male hippopota
Mus can produce "crowd
Waves": it lifts its nostrils
Just above the water line and makes
A loud call that will start
Other male hippos calling in
A process known as "chain chorus
Ing" that can continue for miles down a
River. Taweret had the head and body
Of a hippopotamus, the paws of
A lion, and the back of
A crocodile, and Egyptians
Believed she assisted
Women in labor and protected chil
Dren. Among the ways to distinguish
    croco
Diles from alligators are 1) crocodiles
Tend to have long, V-shaped pointed
    snouts while al
Ligators tend to have wider, U-
Shaped snouts, and 2) while
Both crocodiles and alligators have
    glands to
Help get rid of

Excess salt water, those of crocodiles
Function better, so crocodiles are more
Likely to be found in saltwater
Habitats. In 16
52, Olaus Rudbeck discovered
Transparent vessels
In the liver that conducted clear
Fluid to the thoracic duct; he pre
Sented his findings to the court of the
    Queen

X

Of Sweden, but he did not publish it im
Mediately; in the
Meantime, Thomas Barthol
In discovered and published
That the vessels were present
Throughout the body, and they
Are now known by his term "lym
Phatic vessels." After an 18-month break
From movie acting, Greta Garbo re
Turned to the silver screen as the ti
Tle character of the 1933 film *Queen
Christina*. Greta Garbo's
Mother worked in a jam fac
Tory in Stockholm, Sweden.
Marcus Gavius Apic
Ius's *De Re Coquin
Aria*, the oldest col
Lection of recipes sur
Viving from antiquity, includes rec

XI

Ipes for preserved fruits. Raisins contain

Iron, copper, and, vitamins A and B.
Vitamin A is the best kept secret
Of sexy celebs and top stylists on
Both coasts. According to the United
      States
Geological Survey, the sea lev
El has been rising on the Atlantic coast
Off Atlantic City, New Jersey, at an
Average rate
Of 4 millimeters a year since 19
10; the varying rates of increase are
Due to "residual-post-glacial re
Bound, hydrostatic loading, differential in
Creases in tidal range, and neotec
Tonics." To venture out on the Juneau
Glacier Adventure, you'll need a good
      jacket,
Hat, gloves, sunglasses, and your sense
      of ad

On First Looking into Chapman's Homer
by John Keats

Venture! The Inuit wore "sunglasses"
Of walrus tusks with narrow slits to look
Through. Pinga, the Inuit goddess of
The hunt, also brought the souls of the
        dead
To the underworld. Starting at 50
To 100 km below
The earth's surface and extending to as
Much as 500 km, the
Asthenosphere is the zone within the
Earth's mantle where heat and pressure
        keeps ma
Terial plastic and at a rela
Tively low density, allowing the
Lithosphere above to move as though
        float
Ing, creating the shift of coastal plates

from *Childe Harold's Pilgrimage*, Canto III
by George Gordon, Lord Byron

VI

At the rate of a few centimeters
Per year. Some geologists believe
That between 200 and 1
80 million years ago, the large con
Tinent Pangaea broke apart, with the
Now-separated land masses Lauras
la to the north and Gondwanaland
To the south. In 1875,
14 years after he developed the
      Gondwana

from *Childe Harold's Pilgrimage*, Canto III
by George Gordon, Lord Byron

CIX

Land hypothesis, Eduard Suess
    introduced
The term "biosphere," by which he meant
    "the
Place on Earth's surface where life
    dwells." Mortals, the
Fourth element with earth, sky, and divinit
Ies that Martin Heidegger lists as essen
Tial to his concept of dwelling, are hu
Man beings themselves, whose ability to
Reflect is shown notably in their real
Ization that they will die: "to die means to
    be capa

CX

Ble of death as death." Such was the
    concern
In the 19th century over the
Possibility of premature bur
Ial that many German cities estab
Lished Leichenhäuser, or waiting mortu
Aries, where, laid on marble tables sur
Rounded by flowers, with a ring on one
Finger attached by a wire to a
Bell that could be rung should they
    awaken, the pre

CXI

Sumed dead were stored until signs of pu
Trefaction became visible. The larg
Est bell in the world, the bronze Tsar Bell,
      weighs
202 tons: cast in 173
5, it cracked during a fire while still in its
Casting pit in 1737,
And a fragment weighing 11 tons
Broke off; the bell, with its fragment, was
      raised
From its casting pit in 1836, and

Ode to the West Wind
by Percy Bysshe Shelley

I

It has never been rung. The Girl Scout
    Bronze A
Ward is the highest honor a Junior
Girl Scout can win. Juliette Gordon Low,
    founder

Of the Girl Scouts of the USA, was
Called "Daisy" by her family and friends.
One section of the Compositae fami

Ly of plants, which exhibits ray flow
Ers and milky juice, includes both daisies
And lettuce. Salads with fresh greens are
    per

Fect for a healthy lunch or a light din
Ner. Roman banquets usually featured
Eggs as the main ingredient of

The first dish. White is a common col
Or for vertebrate eggs, due to the cal

II

Cium carbonate that makes the shells.
    Calci
Um carbonate is a main cause of hard wa
Ter. In hard water, soap solutions leave
    precip

ltate deposits ("scaling") that can block
Pipes and lead boilers to overheat. As
Opposed to a metal pipe, a plastic

Pipe will never jam or fail due to rust, cor
Rosion, or scaling, and it can maintain
Its pressure-bearing capabilities

For fifty years. Rusting, the oxidation
Of iron atoms in solid solu
Tion, is a common cause of bridge failure.

Claude Monet's canvases include depic
Tions of new railroad bridges in the out

III

Skirts of Paris, Waterloo Bridge in Lon
Don, and the Japanese bridge in his
    garden
At Giverny. Using computerized

Records of the sun's movements, survey
    maps
Of London, and historical weather rec
Ords, John Thornes, an applied meteorol

Ogist at Birmingham University,
And a team of researchers have es
Tablished that Monet painted the views of
    Char

Ing Cross Bridge done in 1900 on
The balconies of rooms 610 and 6
11 of the Savoy Hotel, while

Those painted in 1901 were ex
Ecuted on the balconies of rooms

IV

510 and 511. In an ep
Isode of the popular televi
Sion show *The Beverly Hillbillies*, Miss
    Jane

Explains to Jed how modern science is
A more accurate indicator of weath
Er patterns than are folk symptoms such
    as

Twinges, and after hearing about the
    chief
Meteorologist, Jed is partial
Ly convinced, since he believes Native
    Amer

Icans to be wise about these matters.
Between 900 and 1130
C.E. at Fajada Butte in what is

Now the state of New Mexico Ana
Sazi Indians constructed a sol

V

Ar marking site consisting of three stone
    slabs
Leaning at an angle against a cliff
Face with two spiral petroglyphs carved
    be

Hind the slabs; the changing paths of the
        light
On the spirals throughout the year indi
Cate not only the solstices and the e

Quinoxes but also the 18.
6-year cycle of lunar standstills. A
Butte is a free-standing landmass, usu

Ally flat-topped and steep-sided, whose
        hard
Caprock protects the soil and softer rock
Beneath from erosion by wind and rain.

When the wind is blowing at 19 to
24 m. p. h, nocturnal

"And did those feet in ancient time"
by William Blake

Migrations stop. Some believe that
Birds can perceive magnetic fields
And that this ability helps
Their migrations, though British re

Searchers have found that birds also
Follow human roads. While all sleep
Masks work to a limited extent,
Sleep masks containing magnets re

Lease a magnetic field that stim
Ulates the pineal gland to
To secrete melatonin, thus
Encouraging drowsiness

And sleep. While in NREM
Sleep, brain waves are slow and of high
Voltage, during REM sleep,
Brain waves are fast and of low volt

from Preface to Lyrical Ballads, with
       Pastoral and Other Poems: "The
       principal object, then, which I
       proposed to myself"
by William Wordsworth

age. Voltage is measured in joules per coulomb. James Prescott Joule realized that a pound of coal burned in a steam engine produced five times as much "duty" (the ability to raise one pound one foot, a.k.a. the foot-pound) as a pound of zinc consumed in a Grove cell. In its crystalline form, zinc oxide is luminescent and exhibits the piezoelectric effect, acquiring a charge when mechanical stress is applied to it. Piezoelectric wafers are used to position the probe of scanning tunneling microscope, used for imaging individual atoms. The term "átamos," meaning "uncuttable," was invented about 450 BCE by Democritus to refer to the smallest particle of matter making up the

from *Biographia Literaria*, chapter XIII: on imagination and fancy
by Samuel Taylor Coleridge

universe. DEMOCRITUS was known in antiquity as the "laughing philosopher." In one VERSION of laughter therapy for cancer patients, patients make "ha ha" or "hee hee" sounds until they start to laugh for real. Lung cancer was one of the rarest cancers in 1900 but, WITH THE rise in popularity of cigarette smoking, by 1970 it had become one of the most common cancers in the Western world. Cigarette smoking became popular *in* England after the Crimean War, during which *British* soldiers followed the *practice* of Turks and Russians, who, lacking proper cigar-rolling leafs, rolled tobacco in strips of old newspaper. Urged by Prince Albert and Henry Pelham-Clinton, who was the Duke of Newcastle and Secretary of State *for* the Colonies, Roger Fenton (*traveled* to) the Crimea to make a PHOTOGRAPHIC record of the events of the war, including a photograph titled "The Charge of the Light Bridge," which in one version shows a cannonball-filled road near where the Light Brigade had been ambushed. Alfred, Lord Tennyson wrote a poem titled "The Charge of the Light Brigade" to memorialize the Brigade's final moments. In 1890, Thomas Edison sent employees with wax cylinders to record Tennyson reading "The Charge of the Light Brigade." Working at THE Edison film studio in 1895, William Dickson made what is known as the *Dickson Experimental Sound Film*, the first film

from a letter to George and Tom Keats,
    Dec. 21-27, 1817: Negative
    Capability
by John Keats

with live-Recorded Sound: standing near a large sound cone in the left of the Frame, Dickson plays a melody from *Les Cloches de Corneville* by Robert Planquette on a violin, while in the right side of the frame two men dance. Corneville-sur-Risle's postal code is 27500. Panama doesn't have postal codes. It takes 101,000 cubic meters of water to fill a lock chamber of the Panama Canal; on average 52,000 Gallons of fresh water are used in each transit (1

from a letter to George and Georgiana
    Keats, February 14-May 3, 1819:
    April 21: "The vale of Soul-making"
by John Keats

gallon = 0.003785 cubic meters). Around 600 "BCE, Pharaoh Necho II" began a canal to link the Red Sea with the (Nile River, but an oracle warned him the project would benefit others only; the canal was completed between 520 and 510 BCE by Darius I of Persia, after Darius had conquered Egypt. One theory as to) the origin "*Of the*" Red Sea's name is that the seasonal blooms of *Trichodesmium erythraeum*, a genus of filamentous cyanobacteria that grows in nutrient-poor tropical and subtropical ocean waters and that can make surface water appear red. *Trichodesmium* converts nitrogen in the atmosphere to ammonium. Sodium azide, consisting of positive sodium ions and negative azide ions (three nitrogen atoms bound together in a line), is the explosive that inflates air bags with 25/1000ths of a second in a car in the event of a crash. 25/1000ths of a second is five times faster than the blink of an eye. To help reduce puffy eyes after crying, place chilled tea bags or cooled cucumber slices on your closed eyelids. Though the Dosakai cucumber found in India and often used in curries is spherical and yellow, most cucumbers are cylindrical and have a green skin. At night, the eyes of a *Bullfrog can glow green*, due to the "eye shine" caused in some *vertebrates by the tapetum lucidum*, a layer of tissue behind *Or within The* Retina, which reflects light back through the retina, giving *Photoreceptors* a *Second chance to capture the light, thus Increasing*

IV

from *Milton: Book the Second*
by William Blake

Night vision. After the Sun sets to 18
 degrees below the hori

Zon, the sky does not get any darker.
 During Nautical twi
Light, when the sun is 7 to 12 degrees
 below the hori

Zon, the brighter planets and stars
 become visible, but a
Sailor can normally still see the horizon,
 and thus still take
A sextant sighting. The planet Venus is
 usually among the
First bright objects visible in the twilit sky.
 The craters of
Venus are named after women, either
 common first names
Such as Izakay or Jane, or specific
 names of famous

PLATE 42

Women, such as Stein (for Gertrude
 Stein), or Amala
Suntha, queen of the Ostrogoths from
 526 to

534 C.E. Gertrude Stein pointed out that
 the ap
Parent repetition in a sent
ence such as "A rose is a rose

Is a rose" does not result from or indicate
fatigue on the

Part of the author, because "We have
insistence insist
Ence that in its emphasis can never be
repeating, because
Insistence is always alive and if it is alive
it is never say
Ing anything in the same way because
emphasis can nev
Er be the same not even when it is the
most the same." The term "rose"
has
Been applied to many plants that are not
garden ros
Es, including the rose milkweed
(*Asclepias tuber*
Osa), the rose of sharon (*Hibiscus
syriacus*), and the
Sun rose (*Helianthemum*). Sun roses
grow well in a rock gar

Den. Drainage may have to be built into a
rock garden to car
Ry excess water from the roots of
alpines: a 12-inch
Layer of coarse coal ashes works well, as
long as the ash
Es have been exposed to the weather for
six months so injuri
Ous compounds have had time to leach
away. Coal is a com
Bustible sedimentary rock, though in the
form of

Anthracite coal, its later exposure to high
      temperatures and
Pressure makes it a metamorphic rock.
      Iron oxide in sed

Imentary rocks gives them a gray or
      green color or,
If present in the form of hematite, a red or
      brown
Color. The archaeological term "Iron
Age" refers to the period from roughly
      1200
To 550 B.C.E., during which people
      began to use
Iron to make weapons and tools, though
      this happened mostly

In the Mediterranean and the Middle
      East; other civi
Lizations arrived at the use of iron at
      differ
Ent times. Most Western scholars date
      the Vedic texts of Indi
A to the Western Iron Age, though there
      are consider
Able differences between Western and
      Indian schol
Ars as to when the Vedas themselves
      origi
Nated. According to Vedic instructions,
      the horse to be sac

Rificed in the horse sacrifice faces east,
      and its head is
The dawn and its bones are the stars.
      The name of the star Gomei

Sa in the constellation Canis Minor, is derived from the
Arabic "al-ghumaisa," meaning "bleary-eyed one," which it

PLATE 43

Self is short for "mirzam al-ghumaisa," meaning "girdle of

from The Rime of the Ancient Mariner
by Samuel Taylor Coleridge

ll. 63-82

'The bleary-eyed one.'" "Lagophthal
Mos," a condition in
Which humans cannot close their eyelids,
Arises most often

From damage or improper func
Tioning of the facial
Nerve, though it can also occur in
Comatose patients, if

They have a decrease in orbicu
Laris tone. The five major
Branches of the facial nerve are
The temporal, the zygomat

Ic, the buccal, the marginal,
And the cervical, and
One mnemonic to remember
Them is "to Zanzibar,"

"Big Mamma Cass. At the Zanzi
Bar Restaurant and Pub in
Menomonie," WI, the
Staff loves nothING MORE THAN

ll. 272-287

Their guests laughing as they enjoy
A meal with friends and fami
Ly. There are 72 coun

Ties in Wisconsin, 10 above
The national aver

Age of 62 per state. An
"Average" is the sum
Of all the given elements
Divided by the total num
Ber of elements: for ex

Ample, 3+4+8=
15, which is then di
Vided by 3 to get the av
Erage, which is 5. The so
Lar eclipse known as Saros series
5 featured 73

Solar eclipses between A
Pril 272
0 B.C.E. and May 2
4, 1422.

Prometheus
by George Gordon, Lord Byron

I

B.C.E. Babylonian
Astronomers were the first to re
Cord a saros series. The snarl
Ing, striding lions decorat
Ing the Ishtar Gate, one of the
Main gates to Babylon, which are
Now in the Pergamon Museum in
Berlin, are a reconstruction,
As is the gate as a whole. The
Brandenburg Gate, featuring
12 Doric columns, six on each
Side, and topped by a statue of
Victoria, Roman goddess
Of victory, in a chariot
Drawn by four horses, is also

II

A famous Berlin landmark. The
Brandenburg Concertos, six instru
Mental pieces composed by Jo
Hann Sebastian Bach, are considered
Among the greatest works of Ba
Roque musical composition.
While most music for the natu
Ral or baroque trumpet, which was
Valveless, is written for instru
Ments pitched in C or D, the so
Lo trumpet in the second Bran
Denburg Concerto is in high F.

The earliest trumpets are
Made of one sheet of metal, of
Ten silver, and date from the Ox
Us civilization, which flour
Ished during the third millennium
B.C.E in Bactria and Mar
Giana. The peoples of the Bac
Tria-Margiana Archeo

III

Logical Complex used irri
Gation to grow wheat and barley.
Deep irrigation, in which wa
Ter is sent along pipes laid a
Long crop rows or root lines is more
Water-efficient than flood surge
Irrigation, in which fields are
Flooded at planned intervals. The dis
Covery in 2005 of
A water-rich plume emerging
From the southern polar region
Of Enceladus, Saturn's sixth-
Largest moon, leads many scien
Tists to hold that that moon is the
Site most humanly-habita
Ble off the Earth. Born by Gaia
From the blood that fell when the Titan
Cronus castrated his father U
Ranus, the giant Encelad
Us was injured by Athena's
Spear in the giant's battle a
Gainst the Olympians and he
Is buried under Mount Etna,
Where he has survived as the source
Of volcanic fire and liter

from *Frankenstein; or, The Modern
  Prometheus*, Vol. I, Ch. 4: "How
  can I describe my emotions. . . ."
by Mary Shelley

ary reference—Pietro Bembo and John Keats mention him. Jorge Luis Borges said that his discovery of Keats was the most important event in his literary life. Myopic most of his life, Borges became blind when he was 55. In North America, legal blindness is defined as vision of 20/200 or less in the better eye, even when wearing corrective lenses. Written in Sumerian and dating from c. 2075 B.C.E., the Code of Ur-Nammu is the oldest surviving code of law. One of the laws in the Code of Ur-Nammu is that if someone severs the nose of a man with a copper knife, the attacker must pay a fine of two-thirds of a mina of silver. Judging by the "greasy" sheen on rock that was heated before being worked by flaking, a South African archeologist has stated that specimens found at Still Bay in South Africa show humans used fire to harden knife blades as early as 164,000 years ago. "Processual archeology" as pioneered by Lewis Binford and others, argues for a more scientific archeology based on the testing of hypotheses according to anthropological research and the scientific method. *Hypothesis* is the name of a jazz fusion album released in 1978 by Vangelis. In nuclear physics, fusion occurs when two or more nuclei join to form a single, heavier nucleus. In cell biology, the nucleus is the part of the cell that contains most of the cell's genetic material, usually in the form of DNA molecules, though a small amount of differing DNA is usually found in the

Nutting
by William Wordsworth

---------------Cell's mitochon
Dria. The DNA in mitochon
Dria is passed on only from the mother,
Rather than being a combination
Of material passed on by both the moth
Er and the father. A bust with the phren
Ological zones mapped out on the sur
Face of the head makes an excellent Fa
Ther's Day gift. Franz Joseph Gall, the
      German
Physician who developed phrenol
Ogy in the late 18th century,
Believed that the combined working of the
      brain's
27 different "organs" formed
The subject's personality, while Sam
Uel R. Wells, who ran a phrenological
Business and publishing house in New
      York,
Later claimed the brain had 37
"Organs." The earliest known book
      printed
Using movable type is the *Select
Ed Teachings of Buddhist Sages and Son
Masters*, printed in 137
7 C.E. A library is a
Place where you may borrow a book
      rather
Than buy it. The library of Ashurban
Ipal dates from the 7th century
B.C.E. and consists of over 30,000
Clay tablets, including those contain

Ing the Gilgamesh epic. Clay is an
Aluminum silicate. Coca Co
La first became available in an all-a

Luminum can in 1967.
Coca Cola is a carbonated
Beverage popular all around the
World. While "carbonation" is a term of
Ten used to describe the process of dis
Solving carbon dioxide in water
Under high pressure, it is also used
To describe carbon dioxide's incorpo
Ration into other chemical com
Pounds, including its conversion into

Sugars during photosynthesis. Sugar
Was first used to sweeten coffee at the
Court of Louis XIV of France, who
Reigned from 1642 to 17
15 C.E. Louis XIV is known
As the Sun King. The mass of the sun
makes up
99.86% of
Our Solar System's total mass. In Ein
Stein's equation $E=mc^2$,
E is energy, m is mass, and c is

The speed of light in a vacuum. Based on
Studies of the motion of Jupiter's
Moon Io, Ole Romer demonstrated
In 1676 that light trav
Els at a finite speed. In Greek mythol
Ogy, Io was raped by Zeus, who turned

Ode to a Nightingale
by John Keats

I

Her into a heifer so his wife Her
A would not find out. A "heifer" is a
Female cow that has not yet had its first
    calf.
A large percentage of the Aber
Deen-Angus cattle now living can have
Their descent traced back to Old Granny
    from
The herd at Keillor, in the county
Angus in Scotland; calved in
1824, she is reported
To have produced 29 calves before

II

Being killed by lightning when she was
    past
35 years of age. Only a
Bout 20% of lightning discharg
Es are cloud-to-ground. Mid-level alto
Clouds—those clouds between 6,000 to
18,000 feet—form the majori
Ty of active weather patterns. Lenticular
Clouds, lens-shaped alto
Cumulus clouds formed by air cooling
As it rises over mountainous terrain, have

III

Been painted by Piero della Fran

Cesca; such clouds are often mistaken
For UFOs. On May 17, 1
974, in Chili, New Mex
Ico, an unidentified object
60 feet in diameter was sup
Posedly discovered and taken to Kirt
Land Air Force base in Al
Buquerque, New Mexico—but no in
Formation has become available since,

IV

And Kevin D. Randle, author of *Crash:
When UFOs Fall From the Sky* states that
         the
Source for the story is unreli
Able and the report a hoax. Chili
Con Carne is a stew made, as its
Spanish name indicates, of chili pep
Pers with meat (usually beef), though in
         poor
Areas beans may have been
Substituted for meat. Beans are an excel
Lent source of iron. A star's fusion of nick

V

El-56 consumes energy rather
Than producing it, so the star's core col
Lapses and then explodes into a
Supernova, scattering the nickel-
56, which decays into unsta
Ble cobalt-56, which decays into
Stable iron-56. Roughly 3
0% of the world's
Supply of nickel is produced by the

Sudbury region of Ontario,

VI

Canada, the nickel deposit proba
Bly resulting from a meteorite
Colliding with the Earth. Typical of
Locations on the Canadian Shield,
Sudbury has hot summers and cold win
Ters. Formed over a period from 2.45
To 1.24 billion years ago,
The Canadian Shield
Was the first part of North America
To become permanently elevat

VII

Ed above sea level. The Poynting-Ro
Bertson effect, by which the absorption
Of solar radiation creates a
Drag effect against the motion of a
Dust particle, causing it to spiral
Toward the sun, means that each year is
About 30 nanoseconds shorter
Than the one before it.
People who breathe in dust from organic
      sources can
Get Psittacosis, or parrot fever, caused

VIII

By the bacterium *Chlamydophi
la psittaci*, carried by parrots,
Macaws, cockatiels, pigeons, and
      sparrows,
Among other birds. The Hyacinth Ma

Caw is the largest parrot in both length
And wingspan. Hyacinth was a youth be
Loved by Apollo, and they enjoyed throw
Ing the discus. Myron,
A sculptor from the fifth century B.
C.E., is famed for his *Discobolus*,

from Preface to "Kubla Khan, or, A Vision
    in a Dream: A Fragment": "In
    summer of the year 1797"
by Samuel Taylor Coleridge

or *Discus Thrower*. Sculpture is the art of producing figurative or abstract works of art in three dimensions in intaglio, relief, or in the round as free-standing objects, and it can be done by carving, modeling, or welding, among other techniques. Minkowski space-time is four dimensional, since time is considered a dimension. The Fifth Dimension won five Grammy Awards for its recording of "Up, Up, and Away" in 1967 and, "in 1969": "the group had a number one hit with 'Aquarius/Let the Sunshine In,' a song featured in the musical *Hair*. The first name of the group formed by" LaMonte McLemore and Marilyn McCoo was not the Fifth Dimension but the Hi-Fis. Though later a generic term for "phonograph," "hi fi" is short for "high fidelity," a term introduced in the 1950s to indicate superior, life-like sound recording brought about by the introduction of $33^{1/3}$ LPs. Unlike earlier inventors who produced devices that could record but *not* play back sound, Thomas Edison's 1877 phonograph recorded sound on a tinfoil sheet that also allowed for the sound to be played back. In 1860, Edouard-Leon Scott de Martinville recorded a short snippet of himself singing "Au Clair de la Lune" and another of him reading from Tasso's *Aminta*, but while his "phonautogram" could graph sound on a surface prepared with lampblack, the sound could not be played back. The main physical source of speech in humans is the opening and closing of the vocal cords. Speech emerges from the mouth. The mouth also receives food, as well as being instrumental in the first stages of digestion. While the term "gastrointestinal tract" refers more strictly to the stomach and intestines, it is sometimes used to indicate the complete path from mouth to anus. The only extant representative of the family *Phascolarctidae*, the koala, an arboreal

from *Alastor; or, the Spirit of Solitude*
by Percy Bysshe Shelley

ll. 106-128

Herbivorous mar
Supial, does not have an anus. As Berg
Man's rule would predict, koalas from
Cooler climates are larger than those
    from
Warmer climates, since the larger
    southern ko
Alas have a lower surface area
To volume ratio, meaning they lose
Less heat and thus they can stay warmer.
    The
Earth's South Magnetic Pole—not to be
    con
Fused with the South Geomagnetic Pole
    or
The South Geographic Pole—is marked
By the fluctuating point where magnet
Ic field lines are oriented verti
Cally. In Euclidian geometry, a
Point has a position, but no size, are
A, volume, or length. If you like playing
With objects, or drawing, then geome
Try is for you! You can make a drawing
Using graphite pencils, color pencils, cray
Ons, chalk, and pen and ink, among other
Methods. Lemon Yellow, Maize, and
    Thistle
Are among the crayon colors offi
Cially retired by Crayola. Maize

Is commonly called "corn" in American
English, though in British English "corn"
means
"The primary crop of the region," and
Thus refers to wheat in England and oats
In Scotland. Popcorn is one of the old
Est types of maize: evidence of it has
Been found in New Mexico in the Unit
Ed States dating to 3600 B.
C.E. Caramel corn is made of popcorn
Covered with caramel. Cracker Jack is
A trademarked name of a popular brand

Of caramel corn, though when it debuted
at
The Chicago World's Fair in 189
3, the popcorn was covered with
molasses.
Chicago, a city on the southern
Shore of Lake Michigan in the United
States, is known as "The Windy City."
Any
Flow of gases on a large scale can be
consid
Ered "wind," though most often the term
refers to the
Movement of air in the Earth's
atmosphere.
Nitrogen makes up roughly 78
% of the Earth's atmosphere, while
Oxygen makes up about 2
1%. A percentage (from the Lat
In *per cent*, "per hundred") gives a
number
As a fraction of 100. In the
United States, a "cent" is a coin worth 1/

80

100 of a dollar. Until 18
57, the cent or penny coin
Was made entirely of copper, though
Since 1982 it is 9
7.5% zinc. Used to
Control downy mildew on vines, the Bor
Deaux mixture—copper sulfate and lime
Suspended in water—was one of the
First agrochemical pesticides. Over
30,000 years ago, the are
A of Bordeaux, a city in the South
West of France, was inhabited by Ne
Anderthals. The name "Neanderthal"
    derives from
The German for "Neander Valley" ("val
Ley" was spelled "thal" until the German
    spel
Ling reform of 1901, and now it
Is spelled "tal"), formed by the river
    Düssel,
Where the first fossil remains of the Ne
Anderthals were found in 185
6. Though often portrayed as brutish sub-
Humans, Neanderthals in fact form a
    spec
Ies in the genus *Homo*. People can
Suffer from brutal depression during
Extended periods of cloudy weath
Er and rain. The term "monsoon" usually
Indicates the seasonal wind of the
Indian Ocean and southern Asia
That blows from the southwest in summer
    and
From the northeast in winter, though the
    term

"Monsoon season" most often refers to
    the
Season when the southwest monsoon
    blows,
Bringing heavy rains to the Indian
Subcontinent; more generally, the term
Is used for any persistent wind es
Tablished between water and adjoining
Land. The origin of the Asian mon

Soon is tentatively dated at 15
To 20 million years ago, and it
Has been linked to the earlier uplift
Ing of the Tibetan Plateau after
The collision of the Indian sub-
Continent and Asia roughly 50 million
Years ago, which created conditions
In which air would become heated over
    land
And rise, forming in its wake a low at
Mospheric pressure area that would
Pull moist air in from the sea, which
    would in turn con

ll. 351-369

Dense as it
Heated over land and cooled as it rose.
    Buttered
Tea (*po cha* or *cha sūma* in Tibet
An, *sūyóu chá* in Mandarin Chinese,
And *gur gur* in Ladakhi terminol
Ogy), a black tea mixed with yak butter
And salt, is a common Tibetan drink
Enjoyed by natives and always served to
Guests, is a refreshing source of calor

Ic energy and helps prevent dehy
Dration in dry mountain altitudes. The
Typical noise made by a yak is a grunt.
Vocalists in death metal and black metal
Musical groups often grunt their vocals;
The style is sometimes referred to as
        Cook
Ie Monster singing. The "Cookie Monster"
Is a gruff-voiced puppet "featured in *Ses
Ame Street*, a popular televi
Sion program for children"

ll.602-671

On the United States' Public Broad
Casting Service. John Logie Baird's 192
6 transmission of a human face is
Usually considered the world's first dem
Onstration of television. In 19
24, Baird had been asked by his land
Lord, Mr. Tree, to move after Baird sur
Vived a 1,000-volt electric shock
With only a burnt hand. Electrici
Ty can pass through human hair, skin,
        and mus
Cles. Keratin, a protein, is the main
Ingredient of human hair. The Ro
Mans adopted the Etruscan symbols
For the *k* sound—C, K, and Q—though K,
Now the 11th letter of the English
Alphabet and used to represent the
Voiceless velar plosive, did not ap
Pear in the alphabet until after
The Norman Conquest, when the English
        lan
Guage came under the influence of

Old Norman, the two languages
		combining
To form what is known as Anglo-Norman.
In his essay "The Escaped Cock: Notes
		on Law

Rence & the Real," Charles Olson states
		that Law
Rence's 1932 book *Etruscan*
Places marks the "terminus of that ex
Traordinary contest, Lawrence vs.
Place." During a visit to Mexico
In 1925, Lawrence suffered
An attack of malaria. The pri
Mary transmitter of malaria

To humans is an infected female
Anopheles mosquito. To help stop
The itching caused by a mosquito bite
Is to apply a piece of adhesive
Tape over the bite. The most well-known
		ad
Hesive tape, Scotch tape, was invented in
1930 by Richard Drew, who worked for
The 3M Corporation in St Paul, Min
Nesota. Saul of Tarsus, later the A
Postle Paul and Saint Paul, was traveling
From Jerusalem to Damascus when
The resurrected Christ appeared before
Him, leading him to convert to Christi
Anity. First settled in the second
Millennium B.C.E., Damascus
Is one of the oldest continuous
Ly inhabited cities in the world,
Though it is young compared to what is
		now

Amman, Jordan, also the site of the
Neolithic settlement 'Ain Ghazal, in
Habited around 7,5
00 B.C.E. The standard time dif
Ference between Amman, Jordan and
        Buenos
Aires, Argentina, is six hours,
So if it is 6 p.m. in Amman,
It is noon in Buenos Aires. While
Until 1972, all time
Zones were calculated according to
        Green
Wich Mean Time, since then official time
Services and world-wide broadcast radi
O times have been synchronized to Coor
Dinated Universal Time (UTC),
Also called Zulu Time, which is also
Used by astronomers to state the time
Of events. "Zulu" is the acrophon
Ic code word for the letter Z in the
NATO phonetic alphabet. In Finnish,
Z is pronounced /ts/. The earliest potter
Y in Finland appears as part of the
Comb Ceramic Culture, and features pots
Made of asbestos and clay. Some arti

v

from *Don Juan,* Canto IX
by George Gordon, Lord Byron

XXXVI

Ficial Christmas snow—in store window
    dis
Plays, for example—used to include as
Bestos. Though the first verse and the
    chorus
Of Robert Burn's 1788
Poem "Auld Lang Syne" ("Old Long
    Since" in
Standard English) follow closely the
First verse and chorus of the ballad "Old
Long Syne" printed in 1711

XXXVII

By James Watson, the rest of the poem
Is most likely written by Burns himself,
Though of the many *who at* Christmas,
    New
Year, or graduation celebrations
Hum the Scots folk melody that forms the
Tune of the poem, few will remember
Verses such as "We two have run about
    the
Slopes / and picked the daisies fine; / But
    we've wandered

XXXVIII

Many a weary foot, / since auld lang
    syne."

Daisy is a popular name for fe
Males: Daisy, Princess of Pless (187
3-1943); Wedgwood potter
Y designer Daisy Makeig-Jones (18
81-1945), and Cu
Ban television host Daisy Fuen
Tes are among the real women named

XXXIX

Daisy, while Daisy Duke in the tele
Vision show *The Dukes of Hazzard*,
Which ran on the American CB
S network from January 2
6, 1979 to Februar
Y 8, 1985) and Daisyjo, an
Animated pony that made her debut in
My Little Pony: the Princess Promenade
(20

XL

03) are among the fictional human
And non-human characters named Daisy.
Strict definitions vary from 14
Hands (56 inches, 14
2 centimeters) to 14.3
Hands (59.1 inches, 1
50 centimeters) tall at the with
Ers as the upper height limit at which

XLI

A horse may be considered a pony. Due
to
"A miscalculation" of the flatten

Ing of the Earth, the first International Pro
Totype Meter bar made in 188
9 was 200 micrometers shorter than
The proposed definition of a "me
Ter." Regardless, the bar's length
became the
Standard measure. The area of

Also by Mark Cunningham

Constelldriftongue. Independently published. (2023).
bl(A)nk. Independently published. (2023).
morfact. Independently published. (2023).
sort/quantum. Independently published. (2023).
A Longer Life. Text with video by Dale Wisely. (2022). YouTube. <https://youtu.be/cSWPjndC7fM>.
Future Words. if p then q. (2020).
"f(l)ights." *Otoliths* 56 (Southern Summer 2020). A 110-piece sequence. <www.the-otolith.blogspot.com/2020/01/mark-cunningham.html>.
"Fail Lure." *Otoliths* 52 (Southern Summer 2019). An 81-piece sequence. <www.the-otolith.blogspot.com/2018/11/mark-cunningham.html>.
multizon(e). With video by Dale Wisely. Right Hand Pointing. (2019). www.issues.righthandpointing.net/multizone>.

Alphabetical Basho. Beard of Bees. (2016). <www.beardofbees.com/pubs/Alphabetical_Basho.pdf>.

And Suddenly It's Evening. Beard of Bees. (2014). <www.beardofbees.com/pubs/And_Suddenly_Its_Evening.pdf>.

Regularly Scheduled. Beard of Bees. (2012). <www.beardofbees.com/pubs/Regularly_Scheduled.pdf>.

Scissors and Starfish. Right Hand Pointing. (2012).

Helicotremors. Otoliths. (2012).

specimens. BlazeVOX. (2011).

nightlightnight. With photographs by Mel Nichols. Right Hand Pointing (2009). <www.archives.righthandpointing.com/nightlightnight>.

71 Leaves. BlazeVOX. (2008). <www.blazevox.org/ebk-mCunningham%20REAL.pdf>.

80 Beetles. Otoliths. (2008).

Body Language. Tarpaulin Sky Press. (2008).

www.ingramcontent.com/pod-product-compliance
Lightning Source LLC
Chambersburg PA
CBHW051659040426
42446CB00009B/1205